FLORIDA
GATORS

BY BRIAN HOWELL

WITHDRAWN

Published by ABDO Publishing Company, PO Box 398166, Minneapolis, MN 55439. Copyright © 2014 by Abdo Consulting Group, Inc. International copyrights reserved in all countries. No part of this book may be reproduced in any form without written permission from the publisher. SportsZone™ is a trademark and logo of ABDO Publishing Company.

Printed in the United States of America,
North Mankato, Minnesota
072013
092013

 THIS BOOK CONTAINS AT LEAST 10% RECYCLED MATERIALS.

Editor: Chrös McDougall
Series Designer: Craig Hinton

Photo Credits: Mark Humphrey/AP Images, cover, 7, 43 (bottom); Phil Sandlin/AP Images, title, 36; Darron Cummings/AP Images, 4; Chris O'Meara/AP Images, 9; Robert Seale/TSN/ZUMA Press/Icon SMI, 11; Public Domain, 12, 42 (top); Irina Silayeva/iStockPhoto, 14; Ann Heisenfelt/AP Images, 18, 43 (top right); AP Images, 20, 43 (top left); Ed Reinke/AP Images, 23; Mike J. Okoniewski/AP Images, 25, 42 (bottom left); Hans Deryk/AP Images, 27; Chuck Burton/AP Images, 28, 33, 42 (bottom right); Bill Kostroun/AP Images, 31; Gerry Broome/AP Images, 35; The Gainesville Sun, Aaron Daye/AP Images, 39; Bill Feig/AP Images, 40; John Raoux/AP Images, 44

Design elements: Matthew Brown/iStockphoto

Library of Congress Control Number: 2013938128

Cataloging-in-Publication Data
Howell, Brian, 1974-
 Florida Gators / Brian Howell.
  p. cm. -- (Inside college basketball)
Includes index.
ISBN 978-1-61783-914-6
1. University of Florida--Basketball--Juvenile literature. 2. Florida Gators (Basketball team)--Juvenile literature. I. Title.
796.323--dc23

2013938128

TABLE OF CONTENTS

Florida's Joakim Noah blocks a shot by
UCLA's Ryan Hollins during the 2006
NCAA championship game.

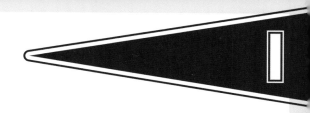

A FLORIDA FIRST

AS THE FINAL SECONDS TICKED OFF THE CLOCK, THE UNIVERSITY OF FLORIDA'S TAUREAN GREEN DRIBBLED THE BALL NEAR MIDCOURT. THE SOPHOMORE GUARD THEN BROKE OUT IN A LITTLE DANCE. HE POINTED TO THE SKY, SHOOK HIS HIPS, AND THREW THE BALL HIGH IN THE AIR.

With that, the Florida Gators men's basketball team put the finishing touch on the 2006 National Collegiate Athletic Association (NCAA) championship. It was the first basketball championship in school history, and it was a dominating victory. The Gators beat the University of California, Los Angeles (UCLA) Bruins 73–57 in the final game.

"It's indescribable," sophomore forward Joakim Noah said. "This is the best I've ever felt in my life. You work so hard for these moments. They're so worth it. We worked so hard as a team. Not only does it feel good; it smells good, it tastes good. I just can't even describe it."

Florida had not been known as a basketball school for many decades. However, it had come a long way from its humble beginnings in 1915. The 2005–06 team accomplished feats that Gators teams before had only dreamed about. In fact, the 2006 Gators became the first team from any Florida college to win an NCAA championship in basketball.

"What happened today with these kids for Florida basketball and the state of Florida I think is extremely significant," Gators coach Billy Donovan said. "I'm happy to be a part of it."

The 2005–06 Gators started the year with 17 consecutive wins, which was the longest winning streak in team history. After a few midseason losses, they then won their last 11 games. In total they went 33–6 overall, setting a school record for most wins in a season.

Impressively, the Gators did it all with a very young team. The only senior was forward Adrian Moss. He was a reserve who played an average of just 11 minutes per game. The starting lineup included

"BOSS MAN"

Senior Adrian Moss didn't play a lot during the 2005–06 season. But he was a big part of the championship team. The team's only senior was considered the Gators' leader. Joakim Noah called him "Boss man." Moss earned a lot of respect from the Gators for being older and also for going through so many trials. He had back surgery several months before the season and then had knee surgery early in the season. On the court, Moss had one of his best games in the NCAA Finals, scoring nine points and pulling down six rebounds.

sophomore guards Corey Brewer and Green, sophomore forwards Al Horford and Noah, and junior guard Lee Humphrey.

Despite the team's great talent, Florida was not immediately recognized as a title contender. At the start of the year, the Gators were not even among the top 25 in the national polls. But they made a rapid rise.

[7]

In the third game of the season, the Gators upset the ninteenth-ranked Wake Forest Demon Deacons during a tournament at Madison Square Garden in New York. The next night, they upset the sixteenth-ranked Syracuse Orange. Those two wins earned Florida a spot in the rankings. And they remained ranked the rest of the season.

After reaching 17–0 in mid-January, the Gators got all the way up to number two in the national rankings. But then they hit a big bump in the road. After their great start, the Gators went just 5–6 during their next 11 games. That included three losses in a row, the last of which came on the road against the Alabama Crimson Tide on February 26.

Florida would not lose again, though. In their next game, the Gators rolled past the rival Georgia Bulldogs. That started an 11-game win streak to close the year. Along the way, the Gators won the Southeastern Conference (SEC) Tournament, going 3–0.

At 27–6, the Gators easily made it into the NCAA Tournament. They dominated once they got there. The Gators crushed South Alabama and Wisconsin-Milwaukee in the first two rounds.

MAKING HISTORY

On December 18, 2005, sophomore Corey Brewer made Florida history. During a 101–58 win against the Jacksonville Dolphins, Brewer became the first Gator ever to record a triple-double. A triple-double is when a player reaches double figures (10 or more) in three different statistical categories. Against Jacksonville, Brewer had 15 points, 10 rebounds, and 13 assists.

Florida's Corey Brewer puts up a shot against Wisconsin-Milwaukee during the 2006 NCAA Tournament.

During the Sweet 16, the Gators trailed 30–28 at halftime against the Georgetown Hoyas. Florida still trailed by one heading into the final 30 seconds of the game. The score was 53–52.

That is when Brewer hit a jump shot with 27.5 seconds to go. He got fouled on the play, too, and was awarded a free throw. He nailed the

MOST VALUABLE PLAYER

Sophomore forward Joakim Noah was named the Most Outstanding Player of the 2006 Final Four. During the two games in Indianapolis, Noah averaged 14 points, 8.5 rebounds, and 5.0 blocks. Against UCLA in the finals, Noah had 16 points, 9 rebounds, and a championship game-record 6 blocks. The Gators got used to those games from Noah. During the six-game NCAA Tournament, he averaged 16.2 points, 9.5 rebounds, and 4.8 blocks per game. His 29 blocks were the most by any player during a single NCAA Tournament.

Noah is the son of former professional tennis player Yannick Noah. Joakim went on to have a great professional career in basketball. The Chicago Bulls selected him ninth in the 2007 National Basketball Association (NBA) Draft. In the NBA, he gained a reputation for being one of the league's best defenders.

shot to give the Gators a 55–53 lead. They went on to win 57–53.

That was the only close game of the tournament for the Gators. In the Elite Eight, they routed the Villanova Wildcats 75–62. Noah had a huge game to lead the way, posting 21 points and 15 rebounds.

In the Final Four, a big second half led the Gators to a 73–58 win over the upstart George Mason Patriots. Then came the championship game against UCLA. The Gators built an 11-point lead over the Bruins at halftime. Florida added to it in the second half to pull away for the victory.

"Growing up, when you're a little kid, wanting to play college basketball, you dream of this moment," Green said.

It was a dream that had finally become reality for the Florida Gators.

"They did a great job," coach Donovan said. "I'm happy for them. I'm happy for the University of Florida and

Florida's Adrian Moss grabs the ball against UCLA during the 2006 NCAA championship game.

all the people that could share in it. It's been a unique and special group

of kids to coach."

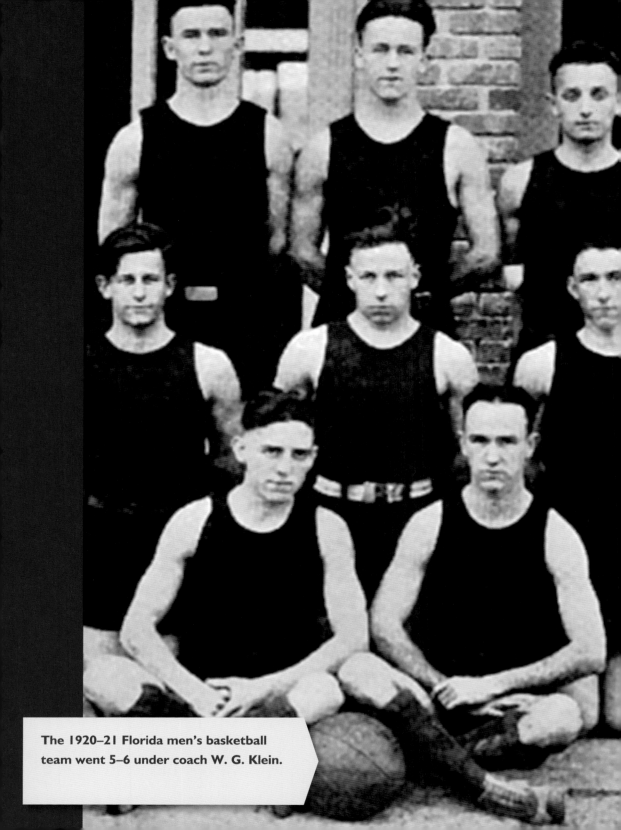

The 1920–21 Florida men's basketball
team went 5–6 under coach W. G. Klein.

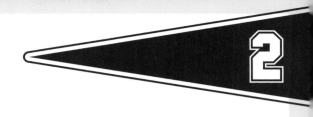

2

SLOW PROGRESS

WHEN THE UNIVERSITY OF FLORIDA WON THE NATIONAL CHAMPIONSHIP IN 2006, IT COMPLETED A LONG, OFTEN PAINFUL CLIMB TO THE TOP OF THE COLLEGE MEN'S BASKETBALL MOUNTAIN. THE CHAMPIONSHIP CAME 90 YEARS AFTER THE UNIVERSITY OF FLORIDA FIRST FIELDED A MEN'S BASKETBALL TEAM. VERY FEW OF THOSE 90 YEARS BROUGHT MUCH SUCCESS TO THE BOYS FROM GAINESVILLE, FLORIDA.

Florida basketball got started during the 1915–16 season. The team got off to a nice start under the direction of coach C. J. McCoy. On December 15, 1915, the Gators won their first game 30–14 against the Jacksonville YMCA. Florida finished the season 5–1.

McCoy also was the Gators' football coach. He might have continued coaching the basketball team, too. However World War I caused Florida to cancel its basketball program for three years, from 1916 to 1919. Following the war, the Gators went through several different coaches.

It was not until Brady Cowell came along in 1925 that the Gators found a coach who stuck around for a while. Cowell coached at Florida for eight seasons, through 1932. The team lost a lot of games during his tenure, but it also found some success. In 1929–30 and again in 1930–31, Cowell led Florida to its first 10-win seasons. The team usually played fewer than 20 games each season at the time.

Two more coaches came and went before the Gators hired Sam McAllister. He had come to Florida as an assistant in 1936 and took over as head coach prior to the 1937–38 season. McAllister had previously coached the Auburn Tigers. At Florida, McAllister became a valuable member of the athletic department. He also coached the baseball team and was an assistant coach in football.

Before McAllister took over, Florida had never won more than 11 games in a season. He led the team to a 17-win season in 1947 and also guided two 15-win seasons (1941 and 1948) and a 13-win season (1940). However, World War II interrupted McAllister's time at Florida. He spent four years in the Navy from 1942 to 1946. Spurgeon Cherry filled in until McAllister returned.

By the time McAllister left for good after the 1950–51 season, he had piled up 119 wins. That was the highest total in program history. Through 2013 it still ranked third. His .553 winning percentage was also among the best in team history.

John Mauer replaced McAllister in 1951 and spent the next nine seasons in charge. Under his direction, the Gators struggled at times. But they also had five winning seasons.

Mauer had three big stars who highlighted his years at Florida. They were point guard Sonny Powell, forward-center Bob Emrick, and guard Joe Hobbs. All three are among the elite group of 1,000-point scorers in program history. The best of the bunch was Emrick. He scored 1,544 points during his time at Florida. That was more than any other Gator

THREE-SPORT STAR

Ben Clemmons was a good enough athlete at Florida to earn a spot in the school's athletics hall of fame. Clemmons played football, basketball, and baseball for the Gators from 1928 to 1932. A year later, Clemmons was named the head coach of the basketball team. He coached the Gators for three seasons, posting a 23–25 record.

SLOW PROGRESS

through the first 50-plus years of the program's history. In addition, Emrick made the All-SEC team twice.

Mauer left after the 1959–60 season. Although the basketball program was 45 years old, the school had never really taken it seriously. Florida's basketball coaches had always either been football coaches or volunteers, and it was time for a change. In 1960, Florida hired Norm Sloan. Sloan became the first full-time head basketball coach in Gators history.

"He basically took it from like an intramural program and built the grass roots," said Norm Carlson, a Florida historian.

In 1959–60, the Gators had gone just 6–16 and finished eleventh in the SEC. In Sloan's first season, 1960–61, the Gators went 15–11 and finished fourth in the SEC. Florida went 85–63 combined during Sloan's six seasons, through 1965–66. That included an 18-win season in 1964–65, which was a school record at the time.

However, Florida still did not become a national power under Sloan. In fact, the Gators never even reached the postseason while he was coach. But his six seasons did get the Gators on the right track for national success. Sloan left the Gators after the 1965–66 season to coach at North Carolina State, where he had been a player in the 1940s.

Tommy Bartlett replaced Sloan and immediately led Florida to its best season to date. The 1966–67 Gators went 21–4. That included a 14–4 record in the SEC. They finished second in the conference that season. Through the first 70 years of Florida basketball, that was the only team to win 20 games in a season.

Led by Gary Keller and Neal Walk, the 1966–67 Gators were the first team in school history to earn a national ranking. A senior center-forward, Keller led the team with 15.1 points per game that season. Walk was just a sophomore, but the center had a great start to his career by averaging 11.5 points per game.

During Walk's senior year, in 1968–69, Bartlett led the Gators to their first postseason appearance. Florida was invited to the National Invitation Tournament (NIT) but lost in the first round to the Temple

REACHING 1,000

Through 2013, nearly 50 players in Florida history had reached the 1,000-point mark for their career. The first to do it was Hans Tanzler in 1950. Tanzler was captain of the team as a senior in 1949–50. During his four seasons as a Gator, he scored 1,221 points. Years after his playing career ended, Tanzler became mayor of his hometown, Jacksonville. In 1951, Gainesville native Harry Hamilton joined Tanzler on the 1,000-point career list. Hamilton finished his career with 1,102 points.

Owls. Bartlett won 95 games during his seven seasons in Gainesville. While he had a good start at Florida, he did not have a good finish. His last four years all produced losing records. Toward the end of the 1972–73 season, fans grew restless. So did Florida's administration. With three games left to play, Bartlett announced his resignation. He finished the season, but the Gators wound up with an 11–15 record.

In his place, the Gators hired John Lotz. He had been an assistant under legendary North Carolina Tar Heels coach Dean Smith. Lotz guided the Gators for seven seasons. He kept them competitive, but he could never get them to the next level. His best year came in 1976–77. The Gators went 17–9 that season. However, they sunk to 8–19 in 1978–79 and then got off to just a 4–7 start the next season.

Lotz was fired after an 82–62 loss to the Auburn Tigers on January 5, 1980. Assistant coach Ed Visscher finished the season as the Gators' coach, but it was a disastrous year. Florida finished 7–21, including just a 2–16 record in the SEC.

After nearly 65 years of basketball, Florida was in need of a spark. The Gators had made progress during those 65 years. But they still had not figured out how to become one of the country's elite teams. To do that, they would turn to a familiar face.

FIRST ALL-AMERICAN

Neal Walk was Florida's first All-American. He was a second-team All-American in 1968 and a third-team choice in 1969. When he graduated after the 1969 season, he was Florida's all-time leading scorer with 1,600 points. Through 2013, Walk still ranked among the top 10 in scoring in school history. He was also still the only Gator to have his number (No. 41) retired.

Although he is no longer the all-time leading scorer, Walk does still hold several Florida records. Among them are scoring average (20.8 points per game), total rebounds (1,181), and rebounding average (15.3 per game). He also still holds single-season records for rebounds (494 in 1967–68), rebounding average (19.8 per game in 1967–68), free throws made (201 in 1968–69), and free throws attempted (278 in 1968–69).

Florida rehired former coach Norm Sloan
before the 1980–81 season.

3

LEARNING TO WIN

FOLLOWING A BAD YEAR IN 1979–80, FLORIDA WAS IN NEED OF A NEW HEAD COACH. FORMER GATORS COACH NORM SLOAN HAD JUST FINISHED ANOTHER GREAT YEAR AT NORTH CAROLINA STATE. HE TOOK THE WOLFPACK TO THE SECOND ROUND OF THE NCAA TOURNAMENT. SIX YEARS EARLIER, HE HAD LED NC STATE TO THE NATIONAL CHAMPIONSHIP.

However, Sloan did not see eye to eye with his bosses at NC State. So when Florida came calling with an offer before the 1980–81 season, Sloan took it. Sloan's return got off to a rocky start. With four freshmen in the starting lineup, he won just 12 games in his first season back. Then in 1981–82, Sloan and the Gators hit rock bottom. They went 5–22, including a school-record 14-game losing streak.

Finally, after posting five consecutive losing seasons, the Gators went 16–13 in 1983–84. They also reached the postseason for just the second time in school history and for the first time in 15 years. However, they lost to the South

Alabama Jaguars in the first round of the NIT. Senior forward Ronnie Williams led the team that year. He became the all-time leading scorer in Florida history and also the only player to lead the Gators in scoring four years in a row.

Florida's first run of great success followed. The Gators went 18–12 in 1984–85. In 1985–86 they went 19–15 and reached the NIT. This time they won three games to reach the semifinals.

In 1987, the Gators finally reached the ultimate stage in college basketball: the NCAA Tournament. Led by junior guard Vernon Maxwell, senior guard Andrew Moten, and freshman center Dwayne Schintzius, Florida went 21–9 during the regular season. In the NCAA Tournament, the Gators won two games before losing to the Syracuse Orangemen in the Sweet 16.

As a senior in 1987–88, Maxwell guided the Gators back to the NCAA Tournament. He averaged 20.2 points per game that season. Schintzius and freshman forward Livingston Chatman provided the

POOLE FIGHTS FOR SUCCESS

Achieving success on the basketball court did not come easy for Stacey Poole. During his career at Florida, from 1988 to 1993, Poole suffered three major injuries. He tore his Achilles tendon twice and tore a knee ligament once. Despite that, he was one of the best players in Florida history. Poole finished his career with 1,678 points—the third-highest total in program history at the time of his graduation. He still ranked among the top six in scoring through 2013.

Gators with some muscle near the basket. That trio led the Gators to a 21–10 regular-season record. However, the Gators fell to the Michigan Wolverines in the second round of the NCAA Tournament.

With Maxwell gone, Sloan and Schintzius led the Gators to a third consecutive NCAA Tournament in 1989. Schintzius, now a junior, was an All-American after averaging 18.0 points and 9.7 rebounds per game that season. However, the Colorado State Rams crushed Florida in the first round of the NCAA Tournament.

[23]

LEARNING TO WIN

THE GOOD AND BAD

Vernon Maxwell is arguably the best player in Florida history. A Gainesville native, he was the star guard on Florida's first two NCAA Tournament teams, in 1987 and 1988. He made the All-SEC team three times. He earned All-America honors as a senior in 1988. And during his four-year career, he scored more points than any other Gator (2,450). Maxwell's legacy will forever be tarnished, however, for what he did off the court.

Maxwell received illegal payments from agents and coaches during his junior and senior seasons. Because of that, the NCAA determined that Maxwell was ineligible during those two seasons. Florida was forced to vacate its NCAA Tournament results from 1987 and 1988. Also, Florida does not recognize Maxwell's statistics from his final two seasons. Therefore, Maxwell officially is credited with scoring only 1,046 points.

Despite that loss, the Gators appeared to finally have their program on track. The 1988–89 season was Florida's sixth straight year of reaching the postseason. It was the Gators' third consecutive season in the NCAA Tournament. However, trouble was on the way.

The NCAA investigated the program for breaking rules after the season. Maxwell told authorities that Sloan and other Florida coaches had given him illegal payments. Because of those allegations, Sloan was dismissed before the start of the next season. That brought an end to the greatest coaching tenure in Florida history to that point. The Gators then went just 7–21 under new coach Don DeVoe in 1989–90.

Kansas State Wildcats coach Lon Kruger agreed to come to Florida before the 1990–91 season. Kruger was a veteran coach who knew how to win. He had a losing record (11–17) in his first season with the Gators. But he

led Florida back to the NIT in 1992 and then again in 1993. Then the 1993–94 season proved to be one of the best in Florida history. The Gators set a school record with 29 wins, finishing 29–8. They tied for first place in the SEC East division. And they reached the NCAA Final Four for the first time in program history.

That team did not have a superstar. But it did have great team chemistry. Junior guard Dan Cross, junior forward Dametri Hill, and junior center Andrew DeClercq all played major roles. However, guard Craig Brown was key. The only senior starter averaged 14.8 points per game.

"The leadership right now of Craig Brown is just very, very outstanding," Kruger said.

As a group, the Gators marched through the first four rounds of the NCAA Tournament. It was not easy. In the first round, Florida and the

LEARNING TO WIN

James Madison Dukes were tied 62–62 in the closing seconds. Cross hit a running lay-up with 7.2 seconds to play to give Florida the 64–62 win.

In the Sweet 16, Florida trailed the Connecticut Huskies by six points at halftime. The Gators rallied, however, to force overtime. Then they took over. Brown hit a huge three-pointer with a minute to go, and Florida went on to win 69–60.

The Gators found themselves in another close game in the Elite Eight. They trailed the Boston College Eagles by three with five minutes to play. That is when Brown hit three big three-pointers to help Florida take a six-point lead. The Gators held on from there to win 74–66.

Those wins led Florida to the Final Four, where they met the powerful Duke Blue Devils. Florida led by 13 points early in the second half but could not hang on. Duke took the 70–65 win. That ended the Gators' season, but it was a season to remember.

"It's fun. It's exciting. It's what it's all about," Kruger said.

Kruger coached the Gators for two more seasons, but they did not come close to matching the success of the 1993–94 season. The Gators did go back to the NCAA Tournament the next year, but they won

GATORS VS. BULLDOGS

In nearly 100 years of basketball, Florida has played a lot of different teams. But the Gators have not played any team as often as the Georgia Bulldogs. Through the 2012–13 season, Florida and Georgia had met on the court 205 times, with Florida holding a 108–97 edge. Their first meeting came in 1924.

The Gators' Craig Brown dunks the ball against Connecticut during the 1994 NCAA Tournament.

just 17 games that season and lost in the first round to the Iowa State Cyclones. After going 12–16 in 1995–96, Kruger left Florida to coach the Illinois Fighting Illini. In all, Kruger went 104–80 in his six seasons at Florida. He had taken the Gators where they had never been before. But better days were ahead.

Florida guard Mike Miller puts up a three-pointer against Butler during the 2000 NCAA Tournament.

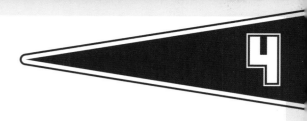

4

BECOMING A POWER

THE GATORS HAD TASTED SUCCESS. THEIR EXPECTATIONS WERE HIGH. SO WHEN LON KRUGER LEFT FLORIDA AFTER THE 1995–96 SEASON, THE GATORS LOOKED FOR A COACH THAT WOULD RETURN THEM TO THE NCAA TOURNAMENT. THEY FOUND THEIR MAN IN 30-YEAR-OLD BILLY DONOVAN.

Despite being one of the youngest coaches in the country, Donovan came to Florida with great promise. He had been the head coach at Marshall University. And in just two years, he had turned the Thundering Herd into a winner.

Prior to that, Donovan had been a star point guard for the Providence Friars. There, he learned a lot about the game from Rick Pitino, who was known as one of the game's best coaches. Donovan then worked for five years as an assistant coach under Pitino at Kentucky.

Life under Donovan did not begin strong. The Gators had back-to-back losing seasons to start Donovan's tenure. But it

HASLEM MAKES A MARK

Udonis Haslem was one of the most dominant players to ever wear a Florida jersey. During his career, from 1998 to 2002, he started 125 of the 130 games he played. He averaged 13.7 points and 6.4 rebounds per game. And his 1,781 career points still ranked among the top five in program history through 2013. Haslem also became just the second player in Florida history to be named to one of the three Associated Press All-American teams, joining Neal Walk in 1969. Perhaps most impressively, he became the first Gator to play on four NCAA Tournament teams.

Despite his great success at Florida, Haslem was not selected in the 2002 NBA Draft. He did, however, have a good NBA career. Signed by the Miami Heat before the 2003 season, Haslem was still a valuable member of that team in 2013. He helped the Heat win NBA titles in 2006, 2012, and 2013.

was not long before winning would become a tradition. Donovan's third season was 1998–99. Few had great expectations for Florida going into the season. But the Gators went 22–9 and returned to the NCAA Tournament.

"Maybe this team has played better than some people thought, but we're here now and we want to stick around a while," freshman center Udonis Haslem said.

Despite their young roster, the Gators won their first two games of the NCAA Tournament. They nearly won the third, too. However, the Gonzaga Bulldogs knocked them out with a 73–72 win in the Sweet 16.

In 1999–2000, the Gators went 29–8. They then did something no other Florida team had ever done. Led by sophomore forward Mike Miller, Haslem, and freshman forward Donnell Harvey, the Gators got all the way to the NCAA title game.

Florida forward Udonis Haslem dunks the ball during a 1999 game against the Rutgers Scarlet Knights.

It was an unlikely run for the fifth-seeded Gators. In the first round, Florida was matched up against a tough Butler Bulldogs squad. The Gators only survived when Miller hit a jump shot at the final buzzer to lift the team to a 69–68 overtime win. After that, however, there was little drama down the stretch for the Gators.

Florida upset the fourth-seeded Illinois Fighting Illini, coached by Kruger, in the second round by a score of 93–76. Then the Gators knocked out legendary coach Mike Krzyzewski and his top-ranked Duke Blue Devils 87–78 in the Sweet 16. With a 77–65 win over the Oklahoma State Cowboys and a dominating 71–59 win over the North Carolina Tar Heels, the Gators found themselves in the title game.

Florida faced the top-seeded Michigan State Spartans, a traditional college basketball power, in the championship game. The Gators' dream run finally ended there. Haslem scored a career-high 27 points against the Spartans, but it was not enough. Michigan State raced to a big first-half lead and held on for an 89–76 win.

"From last year to this year, we made great strides and jumps," Donovan said. "But we've got to make some more steps. I think we'll use this as a great learning experience."

The Gators did continue to make strides. Eventually, in 2005–06, they took the next step by winning the program's first national title.

DEEP POOL OF TALENT

From the time coach Billy Donovan arrived in 1996, he stockpiled the Florida roster with a tremendous amount of talent. Donovan's early years in Gainesville produced several of the top scorers in team history, including Udonis Haslem (1,781 points), Matt Bonner (1,570 points), Anthony Roberson (1,505 points), David Lee (1,436 points), Brett Nelson (1,417 points), Greg Stolt (1,303 points), and Matt Walsh (1,301 points).

Florida players celebrate after guard Mike Miller's game-winning shot against Butler in the 2000 NCAA Tournament.

Then in 2006–07, they did it again. As good as the 2006 team was, the 2007 squad might have been better. It was mostly the same players. In fact, the starting lineup was exactly the same as the previous season. Juniors Corey Brewer and Joakim Noah were the forwards. Sophomore Al Horford was at center. And at guard, senior Lee Humphrey and junior Taurean Green led the way.

BECOMING A POWER

GATORS

GOING PRO

Florida's back-to-back title teams were filled with great players. All five starters from the championship teams wound up playing professionally. Guard Lee Humphrey did not make it to the NBA but has had a successful career in Europe. Six others from those teams were drafted by NBA teams. Five went in the 2007 draft. Al Horford was the highest pick, going third overall to the Atlanta Hawks. Corey Brewer (seventh to the Minnesota Timberwolves) and Joakim Noah (ninth to the Chicago Bulls) also went in the first round. Chris Richard (forty-first, Timberwolves) and Taurean Green (fifty-second, Portland Trail Blazers) went in the second round. And Marreese Speights went sixteenth overall in the 2008 draft to the Philadelphia 76ers.

The Gators set a school record with 35 wins during the 2006–07 season, going 35–5. They went 13–3 in the conference to win the SEC title. And although they did not start 17–0 like they had the year before, they did have a 17-game win streak in the middle of the season. Florida also won its last 10 games of the year. The 2006 squad had won its last 11. In the NCAA Tournament, the 2007 Gators were just as dominant as they had been in 2006. They pounded the Jackson State Tigers in the first round 112–69. Then they rolled through the Purdue Boilermakers, the Butler Bulldogs, and the Oregon Ducks to reach the Final Four.

In the Final Four, the Gators knocked off UCLA 76–66 in a rematch of the 2006 championship game. Brewer had 19 points and blocked two shots. The win set up a championship game against the Ohio State Buckeyes.

With a balanced attack on offense, the Gators jumped to a 40–29 lead at halftime. They held on from there, defeating the Buckeyes

84–75. Horford had 18 points and 12 rebounds in the game. Green (16 points), Humphrey (14), and Brewer (13) scored in double figures, as well. Brewer, who also had eight rebounds and three steals against Ohio State, was named the Most Outstanding Player of the 2007 Final Four.

"I've just been so happy to be a part of this team and play with the guys that I've gotten a chance to play with," Humphrey said. "It's made basketball so enjoyable and a fun game to play. I couldn't ask anything more for my four years in college basketball."

Florida became the first team in 15 years to win back-to-back national titles. "Hopefully we'll be viewed as one of the best college basketball teams ever to play the game," Brewer said.

BECOMING A POWER

[35]

Florida's Jai Lucas dribbles up the court during a 2008 game against the Kentucky Wildcats.

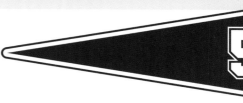

AMONG THE BEST

THE 2005–06 AND 2006–07 GATORS MIGHT HAVE BEEN TWO OF THE BEST TEAMS IN COLLEGE BASKETBALL HISTORY. THE 2007–08 GATORS, HOWEVER, HAD SOME REBUILDING TO DO.

Florida's four best players from the 2007 championship team were only juniors, but they all left school early for the NBA Draft. The other starter, Lee Humphrey, had been a senior. So coach Billy Donovan had an entirely new lineup for the 2007–08 season.

Despite rebuilding, the Gators started 5–0 and went into February of that season with an 18–3 record. However, the Gators got very little attention in the national rankings.

The Gators had made it to the NCAA Tournament nine years in a row. After their 18–3 start, it appeared they would again make it. But they went just 3–8 the rest of the way and did not get invited. Instead, they went to the NIT. It was still a successful season, however. They finished 24–12.

TOUGH DECISION

Shortly after winning the 2007 national title, Florida coach Billy Donovan agreed to leave the Gators and coach the NBA's Orlando Magic. He even signed a five-year contract with the Magic. Several days later, however, Donovan changed his mind. He got out of his deal with the Magic and signed a new six-year deal with Florida. Donovan said his decision to leave Florida was a mistake.

"As long as the University of Florida would like to have me here, this is where I want to be," he said. "For my part, I want to be at the University of Florida for the rest of my time coaching."

Florida fans would like that, too. Through 2012–13, Donovan had a 415–166 record in 17 seasons at Florida. He had nearly 200 more wins than any other Gators coach. Norm Sloan was second, with 235 wins.

The next season was more of the same. The Gators had a lot of wins, but not enough to impress the rest of the nation. Despite winning 23 games in the regular season, they were again left out of the NCAA Tournament. They went to the NIT and finished 25–11.

Florida did not stay down for long. In 2009–10, it went 21–13 and returned to the NCAA Tournament. The Brigham Young Cougars beat the Gators in the first round, though.

It was a disappointing end to the season, but it was also the start of another run of success. In 2010–11, the Gators went 29–8 and won the SEC East championship. That earned them a number-two seed in the NCAA Tournament. Behind four players who averaged double-digit scoring that season, Florida advanced all the way to the Elite Eight. The Gators nearly reached the Final Four, too. However, the Butler Bulldogs pulled out a 74–71 overtime win.

Florida coach Billy Donovan calls out a play from the sideline during a 2010 game.

With junior guard Kenny Boynton and junior forward-center Erik Murphy back, the Gators remained one of the best teams in the country in 2011–12. Boynton averaged a team-high 15.9 points per game. The Gators finished 26–11 and made a return trip to the NCAA Elite Eight. For the second straight year, however, their run ended there. The Louisville Cardinals knocked out Florida with a 72–68 win.

Boynton and Murphy were back for their senior seasons in 2012–13. Senior Mike Rosario, who had transferred to Florida the year before, also had a standout season. Each member of the trio averaged at least 12 points per game. Meanwhile, junior center Patric Young added 10.1 points per game as well as a team-high 6.3 rebounds.

At times, the Gators looked like one of the best teams in the country. That showed in February when the team reached number two in the national rankings. However, the Gators were also inconsistent. They lost four regular-season SEC games after that. Then the Ole Miss Rebels upset the Gators in the SEC Tournament.

Still, the Gators earned a number-three seed in the NCAA Tournament. And in a year with few truly dominant teams, fans were optimistic that the Gators might be able to make a run for the championship.

The excitement only increased when Florida beat its first three opponents by at least 12 points and reached its third consecutive trip to the Elite Eight. For the third consecutive season, however, the Gators' season ended there. The Michigan Wolverines easily rolled past Florida by a score of 79–59.

Although they again fell short of the Final Four, the Gators were one of the nation's elite teams. A big reason for that was the play of Boynton, Murphy, and Rosario. Together, the trio never won a national title. But from Boynton and Murphy's freshmen year, Florida had a remarkable 105–40 record. The Gators also reached the Elite Eight three times and won an SEC title.

"It is disappointing to not make it [to the Final Four] my senior season," Boynton said. "But to make it to the Elite Eight is an honor. Some players don't even make it to the NCAA Tournament."

There are plenty of Gators throughout the years that never made it to the NCAA Tournament. For nearly 70 years, Florida did not have much to brag about on the basketball court. But under Donovan, the Gators have become one of the best teams in all of college basketball.

PLAYER OF THE YEAR

In 2011, senior forward Chandler Parsons became the first Gator to win SEC Player of the Year honors. He averaged 11.3 points, 7.8 rebounds, and 3.8 assists per game for the Gators. Parsons, who grew up in Casselberry, Florida, finished his career as one of the top 15 scorers in school history. He finished his career at Florida with 1,452 points, averaging 10.2 per game.

AMONG THE BEST

TIMELINE

On December 15, the Gators play the first game in team history. Coach C. J. McCoy leads Florida to a 30–14 win over the Jacksonville YMCA.

The Gators square off against Georgia, their oldest rival, for the first time on February 8. Georgia wins 45–24.

Florida and 12 other schools form the SEC. In their first season of SEC play, the Gators finish 4–4.

Joe Hobbs becomes the first former Gator to be selected in the NBA Draft. He is selected in the ninth round by the Minneapolis Lakers.

On January 10, the Gators earn a national ranking for the first time in school history, landing at number 10 in the Associated Press rankings.

1915 1924 1932 1958 1967

Coach Norm Sloan resigns amid an NCAA investigation into the program for violating rules. As a result of the investigation, Florida's NCAA Tournament appearances and victories from 1987 and 1988 are vacated.

Florida reaches its first Final Four but falls to Duke 70–65.

Billy Donovan is hired as the seventeenth coach in Florida men's basketball history.

The Gators advance to the national title game for the first time in program history but lose 89–76 to Michigan State.

On February 4, Florida reaches the number-one national ranking for the first time.

1989 1994 1996 2000 2003

Junior Neal Walk becomes the first All-American in Gators' history.

On February 29, Tony Miller scores a school-record 54 points against Chicago State.

Florida's new home, the Stephen C. O'Connell Center, opens on December 30. Norm Sloan is rehired as coach.

Florida receives an invitation to the NCAA Tournament for the first time.

Florida wins the SEC title for the first time in team history, going 13–5 in conference games.

1968　1972　1980　1987　1989

With a 70–53 win against Kentucky, the Gators win the SEC Tournament for the first time.

Led by a group of four sophomores, Florida defeats UCLA 73–57 to win its first NCAA championship.

With five starters back from 2006, the Gators win their second consecutive national title, knocking off Ohio State 84–75 in the final.

Chandler Parsons is named SEC Player of the Year, the only Gator to ever receive that honor through 2013.

For the third year in a row, the Gators advance to the Elite Eight round of the NCAA Tournament.

2005　2006　2007　2011　2013

QUICK STATS

PROGRAM INFO
University of Florida Gators (1915–)

NCAA TOURNAMENT FINALS
(WINS IN BOLD)
2000, **2006**, **2007**

OTHER ACHIEVEMENTS
Final Fours: 1994, 2000, 2006, 2007
NCAA Tournaments: 18
SEC Tournament Titles: 8

KEY PLAYERS
(POSITION(S); YEARS WITH TEAM)
Matt Bonner (F; 1999–2003)
Corey Brewer (F; 2004–07)
Nick Calathes (G; 2007–09)
Bob Emrick (F/C; 1953–57)
Taurean Green (G; 2004–07)
Udonis Haslem (C; 1998–2002)
Joe Hobbs (G; 1955–58)
Al Horford (C; 2004–07)
Vernon Maxwell (G; 1984–88)
Andrew Moten (G; 1983–87)

* All statistics through 2012–13 season

Joakim Noah (F; 2004–07)
Andy Owens (F; 1967–70)
Chandler Parsons (F; 2007–11)
Stacey Poole (F; 1989–93)
Dwayne Schintzius (C; 1986–90)
Neal Walk (C; 1966–69)
Ronnie Williams (F; 1980–84)

KEY COACHES
Billy Donovan (1996–):
    415–166; 31–11 (NCAA
    Tournament)
Norm Sloan (1960–66, 1980–89):
    235–194; 3–3 (NCAA Tournament)

HOME ARENA
Stephen C. O'Connell Center (1980–)

Through 2013, Florida coach Billy Donovan was one of only two men, along with Dick Harp, to play in a Final Four, work as an assistant coach on a Final Four team, and take a team to the Final Four as a head coach. Donovan played in the Final Four with Providence in 1987, served as an assistant coach with Kentucky in 1993, and took Florida to the Final Four in 2000, 2006, and 2007.

On January 19, 2013, Florida defeated Missouri 83–52. That gave Donovan his 400th victory as the Gators' head coach. Donovan joined Adolph Rupp and Dale Brown as the only coaches in SEC history to win 400 games.

"I remember meeting these guys, and the first thing they said was, 'Let's go to the gym.' I was like, '[Dang], they're already thinking about playing.' When you hear that, you know you're with guys who want to win." —Florida forward Al Horford on meeting teammates Corey Brewer, Taurean Green, and Joakim Noah for the first time. The 2004 recruiting class—known as the "Oh-Fours"—were roommates at Florida and led the Gators to the 2006 and 2007 NCAA titles.

Florida's home arena, the O'Connell Center, was named for former University President Stephen C. O'Connell. He was the school's president from 1967–73. In addition, he was the former student body president, he served in World War II, and he was a chief justice of the Florida Supreme Court.

[45]

GLOSSARY

All-American
A player chosen as one of the best amateurs in the country in a particular activity.

allegations
Claims made against someone or something.

conference
In sports, a group of teams that plays each other every season.

contender
A team that has a realistic chance at winning a championship.

contract
A legal agreement between two parties. In sports, a coach might sign a contract that determines a salary and years of service.

elite
Being the best or one of the best.

intramural
Sports or events that involve students from the same school.

overtime
In sports, it is extra time needed to settle a game.

postseason
The tournaments that take place after the regular season, including the NIT and the NCAA Tournament.

rival
An opponent that brings out great emotion in a team, its fans, and its players.

seed
In basketball, a ranking system used for tournaments. The best teams earn a number-one seed.

vacate
Give up.

veteran
Someone who has spent several years in a job.

FOR MORE INFORMATION

FURTHER READING

Dooley, Pay. *100 Things Florida Fans Should Know & Do Before They Die.* Chicago, IL: Triumph Books, 2013.

ESPN College Basketball Encyclopedia: The Complete History of the Men's Game. New York: ESPN Books, 2009.

Kelly, Greg. Ed. *The College Basketball Book.* New York: Sports Illustrated, 2011.

WEB LINKS

To learn more about the Florida Gators, visit ABDO Publishing Company online at **www.abdopublishing.com**. Web sites about the Gators are featured on our Book Links page. These links are routinely monitored and updated to provide the most current information available.

PLACES TO VISIT

College Basketball Experience
1401 Grand Boulevard
Kansas City, MO 64106
816-949-7500
www.collegebasketballexperience.com

This interactive museum allows visitors to experience various aspects of college basketball. It also includes the National Collegiate Basketball Hall of Fame, which highlights the greatest players, coaches, and moments in the history of college basketball.

Stephen C. O'Connell Center
250 Gale Lemerand Drive
Gainesville, FL 32611
352-392-5500
www.oconnellcenter.ufl.edu

This has been the home arena for the Florida men's and women's basketball teams since 1980.

INDEX

ABOUT THE AUTHOR

Brian Howell is a freelance writer based in Denver, Colorado. He has been a sports journalist for nearly 20 years, writing about high school, college, and professional athletics. In addition, he has written books about sports and history. A native of Colorado, he lives with his wife and four children in his home state.